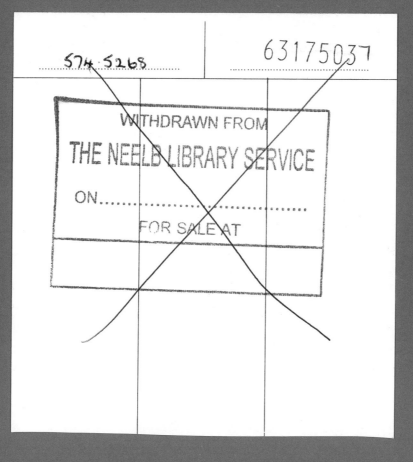

NATURE WATCH

THE
LIVING
TOWN

Nigel Hester

FRANKLIN WATTS
London/New York/Sydney/Toronto

© Franklin Watts 1992

Franklin Watts
96 Leonard Street
London EC2A 4RH

Franklin Watts Australia
14 Mars Road
Lane Cove
NSW 2066

ISBN 0 7496 0778 5
10 9 8 7 6 5 4 3 2 1

Editor: Su Swallow
Design: Edward Kinsey

Illustrations:
Angela Owen, Ron Haywood
Picture research: Sarah Ridley
Phototypeset by Lineage Ltd, Watford
Printed in Belgium

Photography:
Heather Angel 13c, 27tl; Bruce Coleman Ltd 4t, 6t, 10bl, 11b, 14b,
15br, 17tr, 18 (inset), 20br, 21tr, 23tl, 23b, 24c, 27tr, 27b, 28t; Nigel
Hester 5b, 8t, 12t (inset), 13tl, 15tr, 15cl, 18t, 18b, 20c, 22b, 26t;
Frank Lane Picture Agency 7, 7t (inset), 9tr, 11tl, 11c, 12t, 19tl, 19tr,
20t, 20bl, 21b, 22t, 23tr, 26b; Eric and David Hosking 13tr, 16bl;
Natural History Photographic Agency 5t, 5 (inset), 10t, 10br, 11c,
12b, 14t, 16t, 16br, 17b, 17c (inset); Oxford Scientific Films Ltd 4bl,
4br, 6b, 7b (inset), 8cr, 8cl, 8b, 9tl, 9b, 12 (inset), 15tl, 17tl, 21tl, 24t,
24b, 25 (both); Survival Anglia 6 (inset), 11tr, 13bl.

Front Cover:
Robert Harding Picture Library (main picture), Oxford Scientific
Films Ltd (inset right), Survival Anglia (inset left).

A CIP catalogue record for this book
is available from the British Library.

CONTENTS

What kind of town?   **4**
Living close to people   **6**
Life in the park   **8**
Life in the zoo   **10**
Forgotten corners   **12**
Life in the graveyard   **14**
Life beside the road   **16**
Life beside the railway   **18**
Life on the rubbish tip   **20**
High-rise life   **22**
A home by the water   **24**
Strangers in town   **26**
Working for wildlife   **28**
Field guide   **30**
Index   **32**

WHAT KIND OF TOWN?

Do you live in a town or a city? Are the buildings mostly old or new? Is your town near the sea or the countryside? This book tells you about some of the wildlife to look out for in your town. The plants and animals you find will depend partly on where your town is and on the kinds of buildings there are. You will find more wildlife in towns and cities that have open spaces and water, but a surprising number of plants and animals have adapted to living right in the city centre.

Rivers *(above)* can support all kinds of fish, birds, water insects and plants, provided the water is not polluted. Modern towns *(left)* have less wildlife than old places *(below)*. New buildings of concrete, glass and steel provide little food or shelter, but some birds nest on tall buildings.

Small towns *(above)* have plenty of wildlife because the open countryside is close by and animals can move to and fro easily. If new towns are planted with plenty of trees *(right)*, plants, insects and birds will soon move in. Areas of waste ground *(below)* make safe homes for a variety of wildlife.

Some towns and cities are very old. Plants and animals have had plenty of time to become established in these man-made environments. Wildlife continues to adapt as the towns grow and change. Parks, gardens and golf courses form islands of countryside in towns. Rivers, canals and reservoirs provide freshwater habitats for plants and animals. Rubbish tips, waste ground and disused buildings allow wildlife to flourish, with little disturbance from people.

LIVING CLOSE TO PEOPLE

At night, when most people are asleep, many animals are moving about in our towns. Some of them, such as foxes and badgers, are surprisingly large, but they may be harder to spot than small ones such as rats, rabbits and bats. All these animals live in urban areas as well as in the country. Many of them feed at night and rest during the day.

Rabbits need plenty of grass to eat. You may see them at dawn or dusk feeding in parks or in large gardens. Black and brown rats will eat almost anything, but black rats prefer fruit and brown rats like to eat cereals. Urban foxes scavenge for food. Unlike country foxes, town foxes do little hunting.

△ Rabbits live in burrows. The best time to look for them is in May or June.

▷ Foxes live in many towns and cities *(main picture)*. They take food scraps from dustbins and rubbish tips. If pigeons are plentiful, foxes will eat them. Almost half the diet of young town foxes is made up of pigeons.

Pipistrelle bats *(inset, top)* live in colonies in the roof space of buildings.

Deer such as fallow deer *(inset, bottom)* may visit large gardens.

◁ Black rats *(inset)* are excellent climbers. They live in the rafters of buildings in ports *(main picture)*. Their droppings can spoil food kept in warehouses.

LIFE IN THE PARK

Town parks play a vital role in reducing air pollution. The trees and shrubs absorb some of the dust and fumes from vehicles, and trees help to deaden the noise of traffic.

The best parks for wildlife are those that are not disturbed too much. Few wild flowers or insects can survive in grass that is often cut short. Corners of parks that are left untouched are better for wildlife than very tidy areas. Native shrubs support more insects than do shrubs that come from other countries.

△ Ornamental shrubs from other countries are attractive, but may not support much wildlife.

▷ The candle-shaped flower of the horse chestnut tree attracts many insects.

Town pigeons (above) are common in parks, and flock to anyone who offers them food. Town pigeons usually nest on buildings, but many other birds build their nests in trees in parks. The horse chestnut (right) is often planted in parks and along wide streets.

The mistle thrush *(above)* nests high in trees. It feeds on insects, snails and berries, including mistletoe, from which it takes its name. The wren *(left)* nests in bushes and hollows in walls. Wrens huddle in groups in winter to keep warm. The carrion crow *(below)* can be a pest in parks, where it feeds on the eggs of water birds.

Native trees such as oaks and limes support a wide range of wildlife, and trees and shrubs provide nesting sites for many different birds. Old tree stumps and fallen logs are good places to find mosses, ferns, beetles and woodlice.

Many parks have areas of open water. Ponds and lakes provide a home for many creatures. Ducks, geese and swans may live on the water, insects visit the marsh plants that grow at the water's edge and frogs and newts breed in the water.

Birds and small mammals visit zoos to find food and shelter. The caged animals leave scraps of food on the ground, which are soon devoured by starlings, crows, jackdaws, tits and finches. People who visit the zoo also drop food, which the birds then eat. Ducks and geese often use lakes that have been created for exotic birds such as flamingoes.

Small mammals such as mice and rats can become pests in zoos because they steal so much of the food that is fed to the zoo animals.

△ Zoos are built mainly to keep wild animals in captivity, but zoos attract many native wild animals that are looking for food. Some of these animals, in turn, provide a meal for birds of prey such as owls.

△ Jackdaws and other birds often collect the hair and fur from captive animals and use it as nesting material.

◁ Grey squirrels are regular visitors to zoos and parks. They take food from people, and hunt through litter bins for titbits.

△ Tawny owls *(top left* adult, *above* young) sometimes nest near zoos and in parks. They feed on mice, voles and other small mammals.

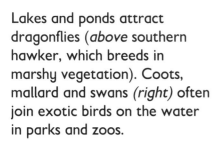

Lakes and ponds attract dragonflies (*above* southern hawker, which breeds in marshy vegetation). Coots, mallard and swans *(right)* often join exotic birds on the water in parks and zoos.

In any town or city there are always areas of waste ground. Some plants and small creatures are quick to colonise these areas. Annual plants that grow and die in one season are the first plants to appear. They produce many seeds and spread easily. If the ground lies abandoned for several years, a succession of different plants will become established. Even tree seedlings will grow if left undisturbed. Sycamores, for example, often sprout up in nooks and crannies between buildings.

In Europe after World War II, rosebay willowherb quickly colonised the bomb sites. It was nicknamed 'fireweed' because it thrives on land covered in ash from fires, and is now common on waste ground. The plant attracts many insects.

The elephant hawkmoth *(right)* feeds on the nectar of rosebay willowherb *(above)*, a plant that produces huge numbers of seeds.

Buddleia *(right)* is quick to colonise waste corners *(inset)*. It attracts bees, hoverflies and butterflies *(shown here:* peacocks and small tortoiseshells). Buddleia, or the butterfly bush, comes from China, but although it is not a native plant it has spread rapidly and insects have adapted to feeding on it.

△ The stinging nettle has stinging hairs and greenish flowers that hang down. It is common on waste ground.

The black redstart *(top right)* usually nests in rocky country, but now also nests on rubble on wasteland in towns.

The garden tiger moth *(above)* lays its eggs on nettles, on which its caterpillars *(left)* feed.

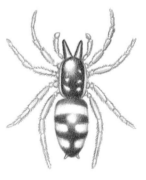

▷ The zebra spider can often be seen lying in wait for its prey on walls in towns.

Graveyards in towns and cities, especially untidy ones, can be very rich in wildlife. The soil in graveyards is often rich in lime, from the church building and tombstones, which encourages plants such as orchids and cowslips to grow. The soil may also be rich in calcium, from the bones in the ground, so calcium-loving plants such as stinking iris and quaking grass thrive.

Insects, snails and slugs in the grass make easy meals for hedgehogs, slow worms, mice and voles. These animals, in turn, are hunted by owls and foxes. Moles are also quite common underground in graveyards, where they feed on the abundant supply of worms.

△ Graveyards are like tiny islands of countryside in towns and cities.

◁ Tunnelling by moles, worms and rabbits sometimes causes the ground to sink, which makes tombstones lean over at different angles.

◁ Red campion grows in shady spots in rich soil. Its flowers may be bright pink or quite pale.

▷ The ox-eye daisy is common in the grass of town graveyards.

▽ Lichens growing on tombstones can be very colourful. The oldest stones have the most lichens.

Yew trees *(below)* are often planted close to churches. They provide good nesting sites for birds, which feed on the red berries *(right)*.

Lichens are common on stonework in graveyards. They are very sensitive to pollution in the air. Fewer lichens can grow in large towns — where pollution is high — than in smaller, cleaner towns. Limestone tombstones support orange, yellow or white lichens. Green powdery lichens grow on acidic stones. Droppings from birds that perch on the stones provide extra nutrients for the lichens to grow.

LIFE BESIDE THE ROAD

You might not expect to find much wildlife beside the road. However, the verges of wide roads and motorways support a surprisingly large population of plants and animals. The grassy edges of motorways are usually left undisturbed by people. Long grasses and flowers hide voles, shrews and mice. The kestrel, a bird of prey, has quickly learned to hunt over these grassy verges. It has excellent eyesight and can spot the smallest movement as it hovers above the traffic. Other birds feed on the remains of animals killed by cars.

△ Wild flowers, such as these blue cornflowers, can grow beside busy main roads, if the grass is not cut too often.

▽ The kestrel *(below left)* is the commonest day-flying bird of prey in Britain. It lives on farmland, moorland and along sea cliffs, and now even nests and hunts in the centre of towns. Magpies *(below)* and crows are scavengers. They scour the roads looking for the remains of rabbits and other animals killed by the traffic.

The field vole *(right)* helps to spread the seeds of wild flowers, which it carries on its body. Butterflies *(below,* small white) are attracted to the flowers on roadside verges.

The London plane tree *(below)* is often planted beside roads in towns and cities. It rids itself of dirt by shedding its bark in great scales *(right).*

Plants that **grow beside the motorway have to withstand toxic fumes from vehicle exhausts,** together with oil, rust, dust and rubber particles. Many survive and even flourish, despite this pollution. Some verges have been colonised by coastal grasses that usually grow in salty soil by the sea. The grasses can grow inland where salt has been spread on roads to stop ice forming.

In town centres, roadsides may be planted with trees. Their flowers attract night-flying insects such as moths.

Remember: do not walk along motorway verges.

Plants and animals can live close to the railway line with little interference from people, because cuttings and embankments are not open to the public. Such areas are often all that remain of the natural countryside which has been lost as towns and cities have spread.

Primroses, cowslips, bluebells and foxgloves all add colour to the rich plantlife beside the track.

Some plants are even able to colonise the dry, stony area between the railway lines. Some are coastal plants that moved on to the track when shingle was brought from the coast as ballast beneath the rails.

△ The everlasting pea often adds a bright splash of colour beside railway lines. It is a climbing plant that has spread on to wasteland from gardens.

▽ The biting stonecrop *(inset)* grows in clumps, close to the ground. It thrives in bare, dry places and may be found between the railway lines *(main picture)*.

△ Some animals can live close to the railway line. Lizards *(above)* and slow worms like the dry conditions among the stones of the track.

Garden spiders *(above right)* hunt among the vegetation beside railways and on other wasteground.

▷ Railways have helped to spread plants throughout the country. The tiny spores (like seeds) of ferns, and light seeds from flowers may be carried many miles in the slipstream of a moving train. In this way ferns and other plants have colonised the damp brickwork of stations, bridges and tunnels.

mosses

bladder fern

liverworts

rusty-back fern

Remember: do not walk beside railway tracks.

Rubbish tips are usually found on the edges of towns and cities. Piles of food scraps, old paper and other refuse on rubbish tips have provided a new habitat for wildlife. Many creatures have adapted well to it.

One of the first birds to take advantage of rubbish tips, near the sea or inland, is the seagull. Other scavengers that regularly feed on people's rubbish include crows, starlings, brown rats and house mice. These animals also feed on the large numbers of insects and other small creatures that live on the tip. Springtails are tiny wingless insects that live in soil, leaf litter and refuse. They usually move by walking, but they can jump out of the way by straightening out the 'spring' that is held folded under their body.

△ Noisy seagulls are common visitors to rubbish tips.

▷ Tough perennial plants such as the broadleaved dock can thrive on rubbish tips.

▷ Springtails are found in damp places; they dry out easily.
▽ Bluebottles and other flies abound on rubbish.

△ Crickets look like grasshoppers, apart from two or more 'tails' which probably detect air movements and sound. House crickets (above) like the warmth of rubbish tips.

◁ The spotted flycatcher has no spots, except when it is young.

The number of flies around rubbish tips has attracted a shy bird normally found in parks and gardens, the spotted flycatcher. It feeds almost entirely on flies, which it catches when flying. The bird sits on a lookout post until an insect comes close, and then returns to the same post to await the next meal.

The brown rat is more common in Britain than the black rat. It feeds on food waste on rubbish tips, around picnic areas and even in park litter bins. It is active at night so it is not usually seen during the day.

▽ The tail of the brown rat is nearly as long as its body.

HIGH-RISE LIFE

The buildings that make up our towns and cities provide homes and places of work and leisure for people. However, to many kinds of wildlife these buildings are good substitutes for natural habitats. Tall office blocks and warehouses are treated as inland 'cliffs' by some kinds of bird. The town pigeon, for example, has evolved from the rock dove, which lives on rocky coasts. The town pigeon roosts and nests on tall buildings. Herring gulls also nest on tall buildings. Urban gulls usually breed more successfully than their coastal relatives.

▽ Tall buildings *(below)* provide roosting and nesting sites for birds such as the town pigeon *(bottom).* This pigeon's plumage is very variable: it may be blue-grey, brown, black or white, or any combination of these colours.

△ Starlings roost on buildings.

◁ Ivy-leaved toadflax can grow in the mortar of old walls.

▽ The peregrine falcon used to be common in many cities. Poisoning reduced its numbers, but it is now returning in some places, where it nests on buildings.

As the sun sets in many large towns and cities, the twittering and chattering of huge flocks of starlings may be heard above the noise of the traffic. Starlings, and town pigeons, gather together on the ledges and sills of buildings to roost for the night. Their droppings may cover the stonework of the building and are difficult to remove.

The walls of older buildings are sometimes colonised by plants. They grow by pushing their roots into the soft mortar between the bricks.

People have always used rivers and the sea to transport goods. This is one reason why towns and cities have grown up beside rivers and the sea, and canals have been dug. In the past, rivers in major cities have been polluted by industrial waste. In recent years, the pollution has been controlled and rivers are becoming cleaner. The wildlife that was threatened is returning to the rivers.

Gravel pits are often dug on the edge of urban areas. Once abandoned, they fill up with water and provide valuable freshwater habitats close to town centres. Gravel pits and reservoirs are visited by many birds, especially during migration in the spring and autumn.

△ Rivers in towns provide a freshwater habitat for all kinds of plants, fish, birds and other creatures.

▽ The goldeneye visits Britain in the winter and feeds on shellfish and water insects.

◁ Once filled with water, old gravel pits quickly become colonised around the edges by marsh plants such as reedmace, and eventually by water-loving trees.

▷ Swans (inset) often breed on rivers right in the centre of towns and cities. Ducks, grebes and many other birds nest among the vegetation (main picture, bulrushes) that grows at the water's edge on rivers, gravel pits and reservoirs.

Most urban wildlife has moved into the man-made environment from the surrounding countryside, and has adapted to the artificial habitat. Most of the animals that live in, or visit the places where we live, are familiar to us. Sometimes, though, we may see some unusual or unexpected wildlife in our towns. It may be an animal that is normally kept in captivity, but has escaped into the wild. Or it may be a plant or animal from another country.

Sometimes these strangers in town are able to adapt to their new home and may quickly spread.

△ These bees have escaped from a bee hive and will establish themselves as a wild colony.

◁ Pets such as hamsters sometimes escape into the wild.

▽ Millet often grows on rubbish tips, from imported birdseed.

△ Cats that now live in the wild are called feral cats.

◁ The green tree frog from South America now lives in some towns in Europe.

▽ The American cockroach came into Britain with fruit from America.

Private gardens, botanical gardens and parks contain many exotic plants. These plants may spread into the wild when seeds are spread by the wind or by animals. Birdseed mixtures contain seed from all over the world, and any seed that is thrown away will try to grow.

Ships often bring small creatures to our ports from other countries. Scorpions, unusual species of spiders and beetles, and even tiny tree frogs have arrived in this way.

Many towns and cities have their own urban nature reserves. They are areas that are set aside to develop naturally, and are protected from building development. If you have a nature reserve near you, you can visit it to find out about the wildlife that lives in your town. You may also like to volunteer to help look after the plants and animals in the reserve.

Many urban areas have their own wildlife group, which is a club for people who are interested in the wildlife in their town or city. You could join a wildlife group and help to protect the plants and animals in your area. Some groups design nature trails that link up important wildlife sites in city centres. Try following an urban nature trail to see local wildlife.

More and more trees are being planted in towns and cities. The trees are not only pleasant to look at, they also help to absorb some of the pollution in the air. See if you can find any newly-planted trees in your area. How many different kinds can you find? You could draw a map of your area by copying a street map, and mark the trees on your map. You could add other plants and any wild animals that you spot as you walk about near your home.

△ One of the best ways to learn about wildlife in your town or city is to join a local club. These people are clearing scrubland.

Did you know?

 Adult foxes take toys back to their earths for the cubs to play with. Tennis balls, rubber balls and even golf balls have been found in earths.

 The black rat carries a flea that can transmit disease to people. The Great Plague of London in 1665 was caused by black rats. It killed many thousands of people.

 In Asia, monkeys and bats live inside temples in towns and cities.

 In the town of Churchill in Canada, polar bears regularly feed on titbits from the rubbish tip.

 In Africa, jackals, hyenas and warthogs all visit towns to scavenge for food around buildings and on dumps.

Where to look for wildlife

Waste ground is quickly colonised by plants, which in turn provide food and shelter for insects, birds and other small animals.

Walls and roofs of buildings may support lichens and other plants, and ledges provide ideal roosting places for birds.

Roadside and motorway verges, and railway embankments are often undisturbed by people, so wildlife can live in peace.

Rubbish tips provide a ready meal for scavenging animals and warmth for some small animals to breed.

Parks and gardens contain a variety of habitats, from grass and trees to hedges and flower beds.

Fresh water in towns, from rivers or streams to garden ponds, reservoirs and gravel pits, provide an ideal habitat for all kinds of plants and animals.

Wildlife is not difficult to find in towns and cities, even in the most built-up areas. Some plants can even survive in the cracks between paving stones, and some birds are as happy to nest on building ledges as on sea cliffs.

Remember that most of the plants and animals that you find will have moved into the urban area from the surrounding countryside. A town with plenty of water, grass and trees will obviously attract a greater variety of wildlife than one with little vegetation. Look out, too, for exotic species from other countries.

kestrel

London plane tree

honey bee

ox-eye daisy

grey squirrel

garden tiger moth caterpillar

goldeneye duck

red campion

bluebottle   fox   brown rat

common lizard

stinging nettle

town pigeon

starling   yew

Spot the plants and insects
See if you can identify the plants and animals that have appeared at the top of some of the pages in this book. The answers are on the next page.

Badgers 6
Bats 6, 28
 pipistrelle bats 6
Bears, polar 28
Bees 12, 26
 honey bee 30
Beetles 9, 27
Birdseed 27
Bluebells 18
Bluebottles 20, 31
Buddleia 12
Bulrushes 24
Butterflies 12, 17
 peacock butterfly 12
 small tortoiseshell 12

Campion, red 15, 30
Canals 5
Coots 11
Cockroach, American 27
Cornflowers 16
Cowslips 14, 18
Crickets 21
 house cricket 21
Crows 10, 20
 carrion crow 9

Daisy, ox-eye 15, 30
Deer, fallow 6
Dock, broadleaved 20
Dove, rock 22
Dragonflies 11
 southern hawker dragonfly 11
Ducks 9, 10, 24
 goldeneye duck 24, 30
 mallard duck 11

Falcon, peregrine 23
Ferns 9, 19
Finches 10
Flycatcher, spotted 21
Foxes 6, 14, 28, 31
Frogs 9
 tree frogs 26

Geese 9, 10
Grass, quaking 14

Grebes 24
Gulls, herring 22

Hamsters 26
Hedgehogs 14
Horse chestnut tree 8
Hoverflies 12
Hyenas 28

Iris, stinking 14

Jackals 28
Jackdaws 10

Kestrel 16, 30

Lichens 15, 29
Limes 9
Lizards 19, 31

Magpies 16
Marsh plants 9, 24
Mice 10, 11, 14, 20
Millet 26
Moles 14
Monkeys 28
Mosses 9
Moths 17
 elephant hawkmoth 12
 garden tiger moth 13
 garden tiger moth caterpillar 13, 30

Nettle, stinging 13, 31
Newts 9

Oaks 9
Orchids 14
Owls, tawny 11, 14

Pea, everlasting 18
Pigeons 6, 8, 22, 31
Plane tree, London 17, 30
Primroses 18

Rabbits 6, 14

Rats 6, 10
 black rats 6, 21, 28
 brown rats 6, 20, 21, 31
Redstart, black 13
Reedmace 24
Reservoirs 5
Rosebay willowherb 12

Scorpions 27
Seagull 20
Slow worms 14, 19
Spiders 27
 garden spider 19
 zebra spider 13
Springtails 20
Squirrels, grey 10, 30
Starlings 10, 20, 23, 31
Stonecrop, biting 18
Swans 9, 11, 24
Sycamores 12

Thrush, mistle 9
Tits 10
Toadflax, ivy-leaved 23

Voles 14
 field voles 17

Warthogs 28
Woodlice 9
Wrens 9

Yew trees 15, 31

Answers to quiz: p2 stinging nettle, p3 brown rat, p5 common lizard, p6 ox-eye daisy, p9 garden tiger moth caterpillar, p11 yew, p13 goldeneye duck, p15 grey squirrel, p17 red campion, p19 bluebottle, p21 town pigeon, p23 kestrel, p24 starling, p27 London plane tree, p29 fox, p32 honey bee.

PRINTED IN BELGIUM BY
proost
INTERNATIONAL BOOK PRODUCTION